Mission Plan

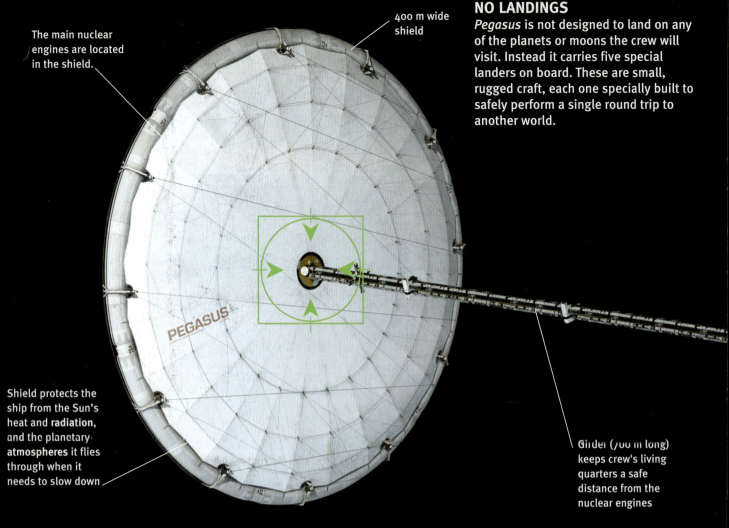

The main nuclear engines are located in the shield.

NO LANDINGS
Pegasus is not designed to land on any of the planets or moons the crew will visit. Instead it carries five special landers on board. These are small, rugged craft, each one specially built to safely perform a single round trip to another world.

PEGASUS

Shield protects the ship from the Sun's heat and **radiation**, and the planetary **atmospheres** it flies through when it needs to slow down

Girder (700 m long) keeps crew's living quarters a safe distance from the nuclear engines

Project Pegasus

The incredible *Pegasus* spacecraft took five years to build in **orbit** 483 km above the Earth. It weighs over 400 tonnes and is over a kilometre long – 12 football pitches could fit end to end along its length.

The *Pegasus* mission will travel to Venus and Mars, then head back inwards for a close fly-by of the Sun. From there it will journey onwards to Jupiter, Saturn and distant Pluto before making the long voyage back to Earth... visiting a comet along the way!

There will be a crew of five hand-picked, highly-trained astronauts aboard *Pegasus*. They will go down in history as the first humans to set foot on other planets.

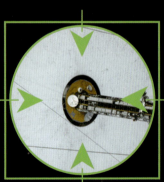

FAST FUEL
These liquid hydrogen fuel tanks power the nuclear engines. On its own, *Pegasus* can reach a top speed of 280,000 km an hour. Helped by the powerful **gravity** of the Sun, at one point the ship will travel at over 1,000,000 km an hour.

SPACE ODYSSEY
VOYAGE TO THE PLANETS

MISSION REPORT

Adapted by Stephen Cole
from the original story by
Tim Haines and Christopher Riley

BBC CHILDREN'S BOOKS/Dorling Kindersley Limited
Published by the Penguin Group
Penguin Books Ltd, 80 Strand, London WC2R 0RL, England
Penguin Putnam Inc., 375 Hudson Street, New York, New York 10014, USA
Penguin Books Australia Ltd, 250 Camberwell Road, Camberwell, Victoria 3124, Australia
Canada, India, New Zealand, South Africa

Published by BBC Children's Books/Dorling Kindersley Limited, 2004
Text and design © BBC Children's Books/Dorling Kindersley Limited, 2004

Edited by Jenny Grinsted
Designed by Nick Avery

1 3 5 7 9 10 8 6 4 2

An Impossible Pictures production for BBC, Discovery Channel and ProSieben
Space Odyssey images © BBC/BBC Worldwide Limited, 2004
BBC and logo © and ™ BBC 1996
BBC Children's Books/Dorling Kindersley would like to thank the following
for their kind permission to reproduce their photographs:
NASA: p.9, p.19, p.42; NASA/JPL: p.30;
NASA/Finley Holiday Films: p.46; Julian Baum: p.12, p.25, p.39

ISBN 1 405 30893 1
Printed in Belgium

Discover more at
www.dk.com

Our Earth is only one of nine planets circling the Sun. The other planets – Mercury, Venus, Mars, Jupiter, Saturn, Uranus, Neptune and Pluto – are our nearest neighbours in space. But from Earth, those we can see at all are just points of light, like stars. They look out of reach, impossible distances away.

Imagine, though, if we could travel in a spaceship to the far reaches of the solar system. Imagine if we could step onto the surface of Venus, see the Sun from Pluto, or go for a spacewalk in Saturn's rings. The technology we need to reach these places doesn't exist yet, but it may do one day.

In this book you can follow the story of Pegasus and its crew as they journey through space. Their adventures aren't real, but they're based on real science. And remember, today's fiction is often tomorrow's fact...

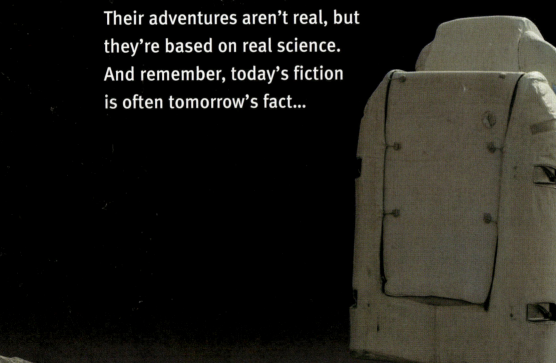

PEGASUS

Pegasus was named after a valiant and magical winged horse in ancient Greek myths.

Pegasus Mission logo

GRAVITY

There is no **gravity** in space. Being weightless all the time is bad for the crew's bones and muscles, so their sleeping and exercise areas are at the end of two rotating 'arms'. The spinning creates a force similar to **gravity**, although it is only half as strong as **gravity** is on Earth.

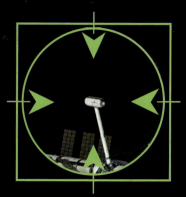

Solar panels provide extra electricity

Living area is made out of recycled fuel tanks, from the shuttles that ferried materials for *Pegasus* into **orbit**.

Nuclear power plant provides electricity for living area

Girder (300 m long) separates crew from power plant

This statue of Yuri Gagarin, the first man in space, stands at Star City, the Russian space training centre.

THE CREW

Left to right:

Yvan Grigorev, Flight Engineer (Russian). Engineer and expert on electronics, computers and *Pegasus*. **Zoë Lessard**, Mission Scientist (French Canadian). Specialises in geology and weather systems. Also in charge of supplies. **John Pearson**, Flight Medic (British). Doctor, expert on Pluto and trained cameraman. **Nina Sulman**, Mission Scientist (British). Specialises in biology and chemistry. In charge of experiments and samples. **Tom Kirby**, Commander (American). Military-trained pilot and navigator.

Mission Control

Mission Control is back on Earth. The team of 300 highly-skilled experts will be watching out for *Pegasus* and its crew 24-7.

The Flight Director is in overall charge. Chief Scientist Alex Floyd and his team will be analysing all the data *Pegasus* and the astronauts send back from their trips to other worlds, while the Flight Surgeon will keep an eye on the astronauts' health.

These people are the astronauts' lifeline.

The only problem is that the further *Pegasus* travels from Earth, the longer it takes messages to reach Mission Control. From Pluto, it will take over five hours for any message to reach Mission Control. By the time Mission Control can reply to the astronauts, a dangerous situation may already have got out of hand...

SPACE DOCTOR
The *Pegasus* crew's health, mental and physical, is top of the Flight Surgeon's mind. He or she monitors vital signs such as heartbeat and breathing rate, and advises what effects decisions may have on the crew.

FLOYD'S FRONTIER
Chief Scientist Alex Floyd hopes the mission will answer questions that have frustrated scientists for years. Was there ever life on Mars? Are there 'Venus-quakes' on Venus like earthquakes on Earth? He hopes to find out...

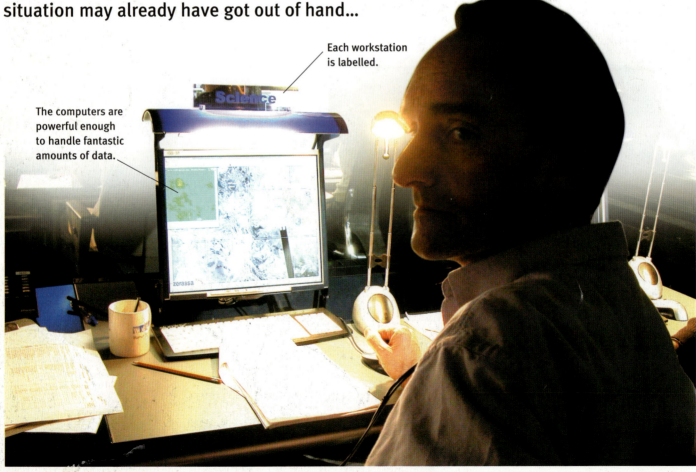

Each workstation is labelled.

The computers are powerful enough to handle fantastic amounts of data.

Key Personnel

1

INCO (Instrumentation and Communications Operator)
INCO is responsible for in-flight communications and the safe working of *Pegasus'* instruments and systems.

2

FLIGHT (Flight Director)
FLIGHT is in overall charge. The safety of the crew and the success of the mission depends on the decisions FLIGHT makes.

3

EECOM (Emergency, Environmental and Consumables Systems Engineer)
EECOM watches over life support systems – such as the temperature on *Pegasus*, and air and water recycling systems.

4

FDO (Flight Dynamic Officer)
FDO helps guide *Pegasus* into and out of planetary **orbits** and watches over the trips of the five landers.

5

CAPCOM (Spacecraft Communicator)
CAPCOM acts as go-between between *Pegasus* crew and Mission Control, making sure all information is clearly stated.

Venus

- Rocky planet
- Diameter: 12,103 km – about 650 km less than Earth's
- Average distance from the Sun: 108.2 million km
- Length of day: 243 Earth days
- Length of year: 224.7 Earth days – a day on Venus lasts longer than its year
- No moons
- No rings

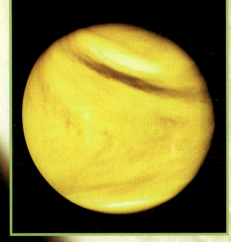

Voyage to Venus

Just 41 days after leaving Earth, *Pegasus* arrived at its first destination: Venus, the nightmare planet. Anyone who landed on Venus without a protective suit would be suffocated by the poisonous **atmosphere**, crushed by the air pressure, and scorched to dust by the heat – if the sulphuric acid clouds didn't dissolve them first.

While *Pegasus* stayed in **orbit**, Zoë and Yvan in the *Orpheus* lander craft were dropped down to the planet's surface. As the lander's speed increased to over 25,000 kilometres per hour, its protective heat shield glowed red hot. The astronauts hoped the shield held out – without it, *Orpheus* would soon burn up like a shooting star in the planet's thick **atmosphere**.

Suddenly, through the dim and deadly clouds, the ground appeared below. Zoë knew she was the first person ever to look out over an alien planet.

JOURNEY DOWN
Having undocked from *Pegasus*, *Orpheus* begins its descent into the thick, corrosive **atmosphere** of Venus.

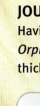

▶ MISSION BRIEFING

Upon Orpheus' touchdown, Yvan Grigorev to perform EVA:
- Collect rock samples for study.
- Set up tests for quakes on Venus.
- Measure conditions in the atmosphere.
- Set up cameras to take pictures of Venusian landscape.

Hot Stuff

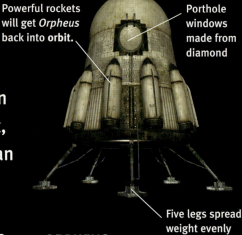

Powerful rockets will get *Orpheus* back into **orbit**.

Porthole windows made from diamond

Five legs spread weight evenly

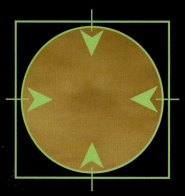

DEADLY HEAT
Venus' **atmosphere** is 97% carbon dioxide, causing a runaway greenhouse effect.

Yvan stepped slowly out onto the blistering surface of Venus. Even in his incredibly strong pressure suit, he knew he couldn't stay more than an hour. Much longer and Venus' evil **atmosphere** would start to destroy his suit – and *Orpheus* too.

"There's a strange, flat light everywhere," Yvan reported. "It's orange. I can't tell where the Sun is. No shadows... It's like looking through water!"

Yvan completed his experiments, but he was tiring fast in his heavy suit. Control ordered him to return to *Orpheus* and, pushing his body to its limits, he just made it back to the lander. His suit started steaming in the sudden cold of the airlock. Venus had baked it to a scorching 465°C.

ORPHEUS
Designed more like a deep-sea submarine than a spacecraft, Orpheus can withstand 900 tonnes of **atmosphere** pressing on every square metre.

CAMERA CRUSH
Several Extreme Environment Cameras were used – each sealed in a spherical titanium flask designed to withstand the toughest conditions. Even so, not all of them could handle Venus...

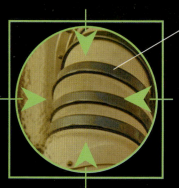

Ribbed sections make the metal suit flexible.

A flaw in the camera's flask caused it to implode.

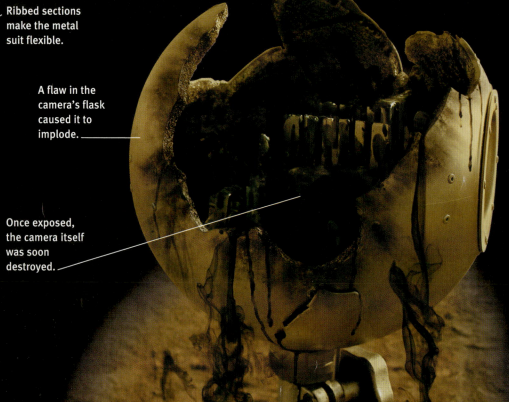

Once exposed, the camera itself was soon destroyed.

HIGH PRESSURE
Yvan's pressure suit is custom-built to cope with conditions on Venus. It is made from reinforced titanium – a metal that is lightweight but very strong. Built-in air conditioning keeps Yvan cool.

▶ MISSION BRIEFING

- First priority is to collect rock samples, so that if the mission is aborted, Orpheus will not return empty-handed.
- Low rumbles felt by Yvan may not be quakes, but thunder or wind. Instruments left behind will give accurate readings should a 'Venus-quake' occur.

Mars

- Rocky planet
- Diameter: 6,786 km – just over half the size of Earth
- Average distance from the Sun: 227.9 million km
- Length of day: 24.6 Earth hours
- Length of year: 687 Earth days
- Two moons, Phobos and Deimos
- No rings

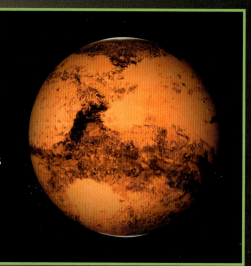

ARES OVER OLYMPUS

Ares, Pegasus' Martian lander with its vast paraglider canopy, glides over *Olympus Mons* – the largest volcano in the solar system. Measuring 550 km across, it is four and a half times larger than *Mauna Loa*, the largest volcano on Earth.

Mission to Mars

Once *Orpheus* had **docked** with *Pegasus* and Yvan and Zoë were back on board, the sturdy lander was abandoned in orbit round Venus, its job done. *Pegasus* headed for Mars, nearly 80 days' journey away.

Tom, Nina and John were excited about being the first people to land on Mars, but also nervous. They knew that more than half the missions to Mars had failed – like **NASA**'s Polar Lander and Climate Orbiter in 1999, or the **ESA**'s Beagle 2 in 2003.

The 40-minute journey down to the planet was a rough ride. Mars' **atmosphere** is 100 times less thick than Earth's, so it was difficult to slow the *Ares* lander down, even with a parachute as big as a football field. The astronauts were tense as the darkness of space gave way to the gentle butterscotch sky of a Martian day.

Finally, Tom told *Pegasus* the news that everyone had been waiting to hear: "*Ares* has landed!"

▶ MISSION BRIEFING

Tom, John and Nina to take Ares lander to Mars and establish camp. Astronauts will remain on Mars for 20 days collecting samples and performing experiments:
• Conduct human exploration of planet's surface in Mars Rover vehicle.
• Search for liquid water – may contain signs of life.

Sudden Storm

Tom was first out of *Ares* onto the surface of Mars. Just as John was about to follow, Tom spotted a four-mile-high dust devil coming straight towards them.

"John, seal the hatch!" Tom ordered.

John and Nina watched helplessly from the lander as their commander vanished in a dusty whirlwind...

Luckily, although it looked terrifying, the whirlwind was no stronger than a summer breeze back on Earth. Martian dust is just incredibly fine, and easily picked up even by weak winds. The main danger was that dust would get into equipment and damage it.

"Now that's what I call a Martian welcome!" Tom joked. His suit would need careful cleaning if it was to keep working properly.

CAMP MARS
On the second day, the astronauts constructed a base camp. Although *Ares* is much larger than *Orpheus*, and designed to support the crew for 20 days, an outdoor camp makes a better work and storage area.

To cope with the Martian cold, the astronauts' boots have heating elements in the soles.

THE HUMAN FACTOR
Many successful robot explorers have been sent to the planets in our solar system. But humans are better explorers. They are more mobile than robots, and can act on instinct.

RUSTY DUST

Martian dust is red because it is rich in iron that has turned rusty over the centuries. Robots will analyse the dust to see if it contains any of the chemicals produced by animals and plants.

Astronauts collect samples using tools with long handles, so they don't have to stoop, and are less likely to lose their balance.

Tools must be easy to grip even through thick gloves.

Protective inner lining

Titanium case with secure fasteners

TOOLS OF THE TRADE

All equipment is designed to be used easily by astronauts in bulky pressure suits in low **gravity**. Similar equipment was used on the Moon in the 1960s and 1970s.

Martian Menaces

Five days after landing, the astronauts took a trip in the Mars Rover with 'Charlie' – a very special robot designed to sniff out liquid water beneath the Martian surface. The robot would float down by balloon and search at the bottom of *Valles Marineris*, a massive chasm in the Martian landscape seven kilometres deep.

"Makes the Grand Canyon look like a scratch!" John remarked.

'CHARLIE'
'Charlie' – also known as MVP-14 – is a robot fitted with sensors that detect possible water beneath the ground. If it thinks it has found water, a drilling probe extends to collect a sample.

CARS ON MARS
The Mars Rover cost $2 billion to adapt from similar craft used on the Moon. It can travel for 10 hours without recharging at a top speed of 14.5 km per hour.

Before they could release 'Charlie', Mission Control warned of a **solar flare** coming. This burst of extra sunrays doesn't bother people on Earth, but because Mars has a thinner **atmosphere** and no magnetic field, the astronauts could be exposed to harmful **radiation**. They retreated quickly back to base.

Several long, frustrating days passed before Tom, John and Nina could risk sending 'Charlie' down to the canyon floor. But when they finally did, they got a real result.

"Charlie's drinking!" cried Nina.

As the astronauts celebrated, they knew their time on Mars was coming to an end. Their next destination was Jupiter – shining in the night sky like a bright beacon.

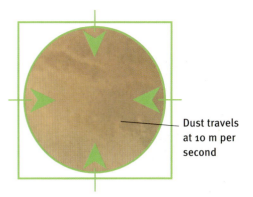

Dust travels at 10 m per second

BLOWN AWAY
Strong winds surge from one end of the canyon to the other, carrying tonnes of dust. This dust storm is 500 km wide.

INCREDIBLE CANYON
Valles Marineris is an awe-inspiring sight – almost as deep as Mount Everest is high, and 4,000 km long. It stretches so far across Mars that while one end is in daylight, the other end is in darkness.

▶ MISSION BRIEFING
• If dust storm blows up, abandon area immediately.
• Working close to canyon edge in zero visibility is NOT advised.

Sun Swing

Jupiter was currently on the other side of the solar system from Mars, and the quickest way to get there was to speed past the Sun. The crew knew this was dangerous. The Sun is a giant ball of burning gas generating not only heat and light, but also deadly **radiation**. *Pegasus* would generate a protective magnetic shield, but some **radiation** might get through. And if a **solar flare** went up unexpectedly near *Pegasus,* at such close range nothing could save them.

It was sweltering on board as *Pegasus* neared the Sun. Cameras and computers malfunctioned, unable to cope with the strength of the Sun's overwhelming energies.

"Good luck, guys," said Tom.

"Our readings are fine so far," said John, hoping he sounded less nervous than he felt.

Everyone was relieved when *Pegasus* made it past and hurtled on to Jupiter – only seven months and 770 million kilometres away.

THE POWER OF LIGHT
Pulled by the Sun's gravity (28 times that of Earth), *Pegasus* zooms past the Sun at over 1,000,000 km per hour.

> **MISSION BRIEFING**
> - Fly through Sun's outer atmosphere.
> - Collect samples and transmit pictures.
> - Analyse data from first close contact with a star.

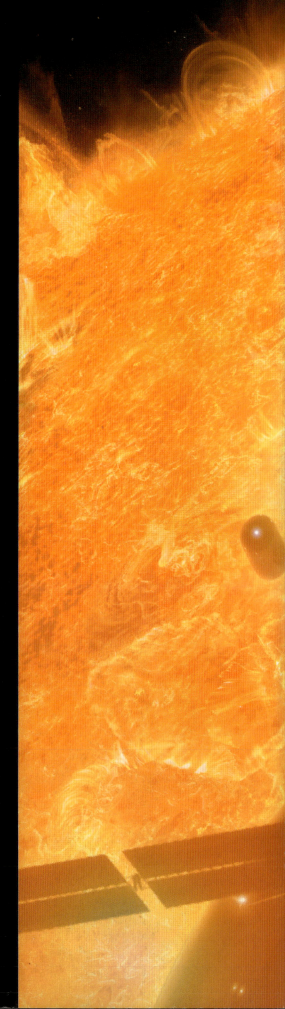

The Sun

- Star
- Diameter: 1,392,000 km – over one million planets the size of Earth could fit inside it.
- All the planets, comets and asteroids in our solar system are in **orbit** around it.
- It is five billion years old.
- Raging nuclear reactions at its core convert hydrogen into helium at a rate of 600 million tonnes per second, generating light, heat and **radiation**.
- It will start to run low on fuel in about five billion years.

Life on Pegasus

The long trip to Jupiter saw the crew having to cope with one of their biggest challenges: the crushing boredom of deep space travel. With only the endless blackness of space outside, *Pegasus* became a kind of prison built for five – with no visitors.

The size of *Pegasus* meant that maintenance and repairs took up a lot of time. Everyone also exercised three hours a day in half-Earth 'gravity' – otherwise their bones and muscles would weaken. As Tom said, "Use them or lose them!"

When they weren't fixing up *Pegasus*, working out or doing experiments on the samples they had collected, the astronauts could send emails, watch TV transmitted from Earth, or play music chosen from the thousands of songs stored as MP3 files. And each of them had a diary camera to record their private feelings.

COMPUTER LOCK
Laptops can be clamped in place and networked with the main computer system.

FOOD AND DRINK
All the water on *Pegasus* is recycled. Most food is dried, but some is grown on board, like these tomatoes. They grow in special fluid instead of soil.

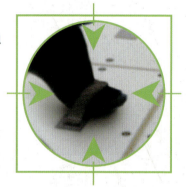

FEET ON THE FLOOR
Special footholds help the crew keep themselves steady while working in zero **gravity**.

ONLY HOME
Zoë sold her house on Earth to help her accept *Pegasus* as her only home for the six-year mission.

Pegasus' rotating 'arms' provide half-Earth 'gravity' in sleeping and exercise areas – except when the motor is turned off for repairs!

Many books are stored in *Pegasus'* computers, but Zoë prefers bound books. They're easier to read than printouts, especially in zero **gravity**. But she could only bring 20 of her favourite novels.

OVHD

HATCH EXIT

STBD

TO N

Space Rocks!

TIME LAG
The further away *Pegasus* travels from Earth, the longer it takes for signals to reach Mission Control. This can lead to agonising delays.

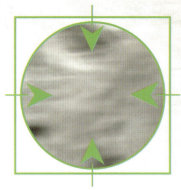

BELTING ALONG
Scientists estimate there are 1.4 million rocks in the asteroid belt lying between Mars and Jupiter. They may have come from a planet that broke up billions of years ago. Some of the asteroids are no bigger than a pebble, while others are the size of Spain.

NAME BLAME
The crew were angry that Mission Control had risked their lives. They named the two asteroids Hubris (meaning 'false pride') and Catastrophe ('total disaster').

All was quiet on board, when an alarm blared out. *Pegasus* was passing through the asteroid belt – and something was heading their way. Yvan reached a grim conclusion: two asteroids with a total weight of 224 billion tonnes would pass within a kilometre of *Pegasus* – in 55 minutes!

"We need a course correction," said Yvan, submitting his findings to Earth.

It took a tense 38 minutes for Mission Control's reply to reach *Pegasus* – and when it did, the crew were ordered to stay on course. Mission Control believed the asteroids would come no closer than ten kilometres.

Tom shrugged nervously. "They've got better data."

The crew watched, helpless… as the asteroids scraped past *Pegasus* at a distance of just 920 metres.

"Better get out and check the paintwork," said Yvan, shakily. "Are we insured?"

> **MISSION BRIEFING supplemental**
> Do NOT correct course:
> • Perform fly-by of double asteroid.
> • Measure size, map major markings.
> • Scan composition – learn what they are made of.

Journey to Jupiter

FEEL THE BURN

As *Pegasus* skims Jupiter's cloud tops, its heat shield reaches 2,900°C. Jupiter is a gigantic ball of different types of gas and liquid, clinging in great layers around a rocky core.

Pegasus was travelling at 160,000 kilometres per hour, and the crew needed to slow the spaceship down before it could fall into **orbit** around Jupiter. If they flew shield-first into the planet's cloud tops, the friction between *Pegasus* and Jupiter's thick **atmosphere** would act like a powerful brake.

   The spacecraft seemed to scream as it slammed into the gas giant. Its shield burnt white hot as it tore through the clouds...

Then, suddenly, it was over. *Pegasus* was in orbit! But the astronauts' relief didn't last long once Yvan looked at Io, Jupiter's third largest moon, through *Pegasus'* telescope.

"Can you see the landing site?" asked Tom.

Yvan looked at him grimly. "A volcano just erupted there. We don't *have* a landing site!"

With the ideal site swamped by ash, Zoë had to land somewhere more dangerous. As she prepared to touch down on Io in the *Hermes* lander, everyone hoped for the best...

Jupiter

- Gas giant
- Diameter: 142,980 km – you could fit 1,300 Earths inside Jupiter
- Average distance from the Sun: 778.6 million km
- Length of day: 9.9 Earth hours
- Length of year: 11.85 Earth years
- Over 60 moons
- Three thin, barely visible rings

▶ MISSION BRIEFING

- The main danger round Jupiter is its deadly radiation belts.
- Activate magnetic shield and keep to better-protected parts of Pegasus.
- The radiation generates natural radio waves. Crew to tune in and listen to Radio Jupiter! It sounds like woodpeckers tapping trees beside a creepy crashing ocean.

Panic on Io

Zoë stepped onto a patchwork of lava. Sulphur crystals crunched beneath her feet like fresh snow. Bigger than anything she had ever seen, Jupiter dominated the sky.

Awestruck, Zoë started collecting samples. But her suit was so awkward, she found it hard to move around. Long minutes dragged by.

John's voice crackled inside her helmet. "Breathe slowly and steadily, Zoë..."

But it was no good. The suit was just too awkward, and Zoë was having to work too hard. Her heart was beating too fast, and she was using up her oxygen too quickly.

"Get back to the lander, Zoë!" ordered Tom. "Now!"

Dumping the precious samples, Zoë barely made it back inside before collapsing. The crew had to steer *Hermes* back to *Pegasus* by remote control.

ERUPTION
Io has low **gravity** and no **atmosphere**, so volcanic eruptions look different from those on Earth. Ash spurts out at up to 2,000 m per second, then forms an enormous dome as it falls.

Sulphur gives Io's lava its yellow colour.

LAVA SCULPTURES
Lava is rock that has become so hot it has melted. Io's volcanoes are very hot, but the rest of the moon is very cold. Once an eruption has occurred, the lava cools quickly into strangely-shaped stacks.

Oversized helmet with tinted visor reduces glare for increased visibility

SUITS YOU
Zoë's **EVA** suit has a thick protective lining that will, for a time, absorb harmful **radiation**. It also generates its own magnetic field to keep killer rays outside the suit.

- New landing site is in an area where radiation levels can change quickly.
- Flight Surgeon advises that Zoë should spend no longer than four hours on Io and that conditions should be monitored closely.

Deep Ice, Sky High

Zoë was bitterly disappointed. She felt she had let everyone down – including herself.

"They should have sent a robot," she told her diary-cam sadly. "Cheaper and more effective. All I did was scare everyone half to death."

But the mission had to go on, and the next job for *Pegasus* was to pick up the *Shackleton* probe – a robotic probe that had left Earth before *Pegasus* did, and had been studying the frozen moon of Europa.

BENEATH THE ICE

Europa, the fourth largest of Jupiter's moons, looks almost completely flat. It is thought that the moon is covered with ice, beneath which there is an ocean of salt water over 100 km deep. After Mars (and Earth, of course), this ocean is the most likely place to find life in our solar system.

Eight kilometres above the clouds, Jupiter's **atmosphere** may be cool enough for phosphorus gas to condense into a liquid – creating the red colour.

▶ MISSION BRIEFING

- Europa's surface ice is too thick to drill through, but Shackleton has taken samples from an area hit by an asteroid, where the ice is thinner.
- Pegasus to dock with probe and recover samples.

JUNO
This nuclear-powered robotic probe will cruise the cloudscapes of Jupiter for months. It will give daily weather readings for about 100 days before Jupiter's heat and pressure destroy it.

Pegasus had also launched a probe of its own – *Juno*, designed to travel into Jupiter's Great Red Spot. The probe powered through the cascading clouds at speeds of almost 10,000 kilometres per hour, busily taking readings.

John, though, was looking quiet and drawn. He had just received some terrible news.

SEEING RED
Jupiter's Great Red Spot is a hurricane twice the size of Earth, and towering about eight kilometres above Jupiter's cloud tops. The storm has been raging for hundreds of years: it was first sighted in 1665.

Saturn

- Gas giant
- Diameter: 120,540 km – you could fit 750 Earths inside Saturn
- Average distance from the Sun: 1.4 billion km
- Length of day: 10.7 Earth hours
- Length of year: 29.4 Earth years
- 30 moons
- Seven dazzling rings

A Stop at Saturn

Ten months away, across two billion kilometres of space, lay Saturn, *Pegasus'* next stop. But John wasn't sure he'd make it. He was dying, his body poisoned by **radiation** from the Sun. "The others are OK, thank goodness," he told his diary-cam. "I was just unlucky." Gradually, Saturn and its incredible rings came into sharp focus through *Pegasus'* telescope. John willed himself to hold on until they arrived. More than anything, he wanted to see Saturn with his own eyes.

It was impossible to carry on as if nothing was wrong, but Tom, Nina, Yvan and Zoë tried to stay strong for John's sake.

At last, *Pegasus* neared Saturn. "The most beautiful place I've been," John murmured. "I could watch it forever."

RINGED WORLD
Pegasus fires its engines beside the gas giant Saturn, the solar system's second largest planet.

▶ MISSION BRIEFING
- Pegasus to take up position within the rings of Saturn.
- Nina Sulman to perform EVA and take samples from the rings for study.

Glittering Rings

Using a jet pack, Nina steered herself towards each ring fragment she wanted to take back for study. The icy particles ranged in size from grains of dust to chunks the size of a bus. And there she was, floating silently in the depths of space amongst their glittering beauty. She looked down, and all she could see was the broad, striped face of Saturn staring back at her. *Pegasus*, her home now for more than two years, seemed tiny in comparison. It was a breathtaking, incredible moment.

Then Zoë's voice burst into her helmet, shattering the silence. "You have to come in, Nina. Now," said Zoë. She sounded like she'd been crying.

Nina knew there was bad news waiting for her, back on board.

Rings divide into five major bands and two minor ones.

RING DIVISION
Saturn's rings are made up of tumbling lumps of ice and rock – possibly the remains of a moon or comet torn apart by Saturn's **gravity**.

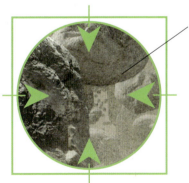

As the chunks knock against each other they are slowly worn away. In a few hundred million years, Saturn's rings might be no more.

SPREAD THIN
Saturn's rings are 272,500 km wide, but the amount of material would barely make a moon 400 km across. To get an idea of how thinly the material is spread, imagine tissue paper covering a football field!

OUT ON A SPACEWALK
On her spacewalk, Nina is not tied to *Pegasus* in any way. She moves around freely using a jet pack on her back. Anyone leaving the ship puts themselves at great risk, and spacewalks require a lot of training and planning.

Silent Departure

Dr John Pearson passed away on day 748 of the mission. Because the water on board *Pegasus* is recycled, it was impossible to treat his illness – the strong drugs he needed would have polluted the other astronauts' drinking water.

STARLIGHT EXTREME
Flying so close to the Sun was an intense experience – and, for John, a fatal one. Even 50 days away from *Pegasus*' closest approach, the glare through the ship's windows was almost unbearable.

The crew went offline for the next 24 hours, breaking contact with Mission Control. During that time, Tom put on his spacesuit. He wasn't supposed to leave *Pegasus*, but he felt he must – there was something he needed to take care of. As he floated out into the stark blackness of space, he carefully held a long silver bag. Inside it was John's weightless body.

Gently, Tom pushed the bag towards Saturn's rings. It started to tumble, slowly, like the frozen rocks all around. Now, John would remain a tiny part of the most beautiful sight in the solar system – the perfect resting place for a brave astronaut.

FINEST HOURS
John was proudest of his time on Mars. Back on Earth, he had said that giving up six years of his life wasn't giving up anything. "It's you lot I feel sorry for," he had said. "You'll see the pictures but you'll just never know."

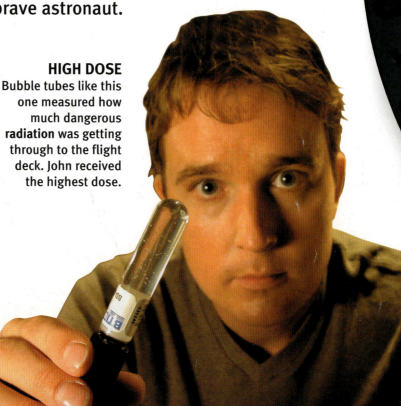

HIGH DOSE
Bubble tubes like this one measured how much dangerous **radiation** was getting through to the flight deck. John received the highest dose.

Crisis Point

The crew of *Pegasus* had been away for over two years. To travel on to Pluto would add another three years to the mission – and John wasn't coming back at all. As they carried out repairs and refuelled over Titan, Saturn's largest moon, Tom, Nina, Yvan and Zoë wondered whether they could bring themselves to continue. Should they just cut their losses and head home?

In the end, the decision was unanimous. As Tom said, "You don't climb halfway up Mount Everest and say the view is good enough. Not when someone died to get you there."

They began testing some of the samples they had collected, although the plan had been to wait and study them more closely on Earth.

"If John taught us anything, it's not to make too many plans," Nina said. "We might not be coming home."

OUT FOR REPAIRS
Radiation and dust particles continually damage *Pegasus*' hull. The only way to make repairs is by spacewalking outside the ship.

FILLING UP
Fuel tanks have been fired off to key pickup points ahead of *Pegasus*. Each is full of hydrogen gas and is 500 m wide and 3 km long – more than twice the length of *Pegasus*!

LIFE?
When Nina tested the Martian soil samples, she discovered traces of plant life. But Mission Control suspected the sample had been contaminated by something on *Pegasus*. She would have to wait till they were back on Earth to know for sure if there had once been life on Mars.

TITANIC ENCOUNTER
Titan is Saturn's largest and most mysterious moon. A hazy orange **atmosphere** hides the surface, but scientists believe all the elements needed for life may be found there in deep freeze.

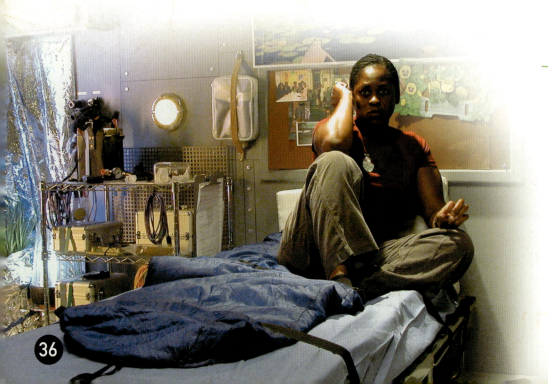

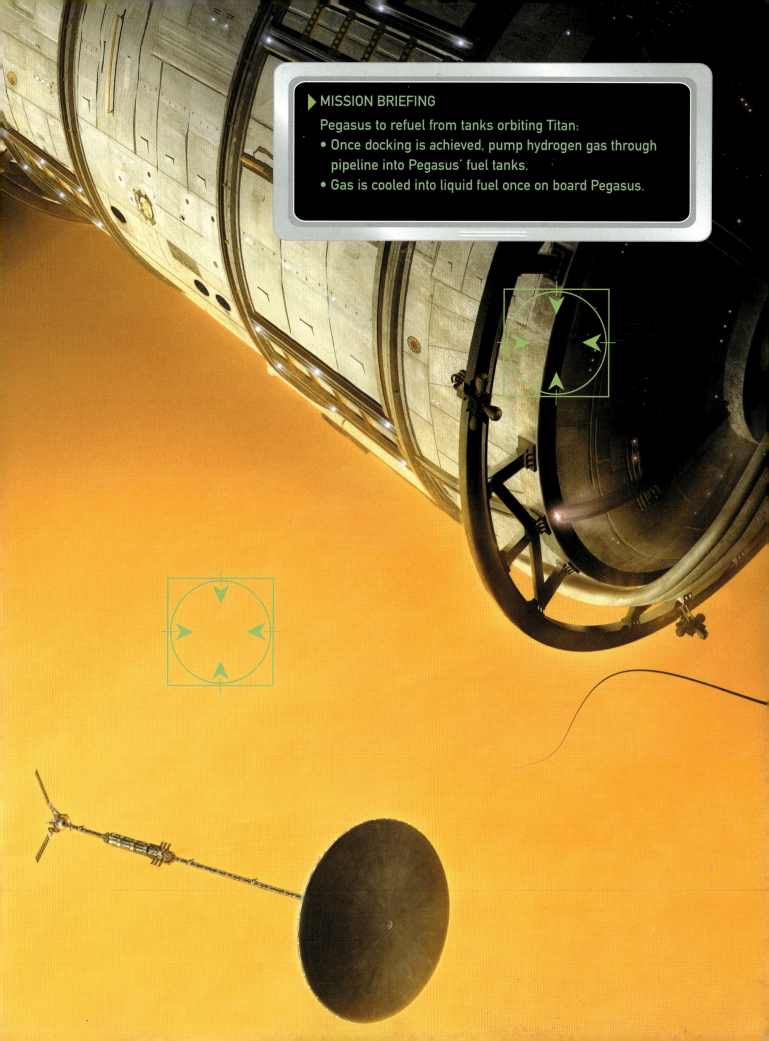

Pegasus to refuel from tanks orbiting Titan:

- Once docking is achieved, pump hydrogen gas through pipeline into Pegasus' fuel tanks.
- Gas is cooled into liquid fuel once on board Pegasus.

▶ MISSION BRIEFING

In absence of Pluto expert John, Yvan and Tom to undertake Pluto expedition:

• Expedition to last 15 days.
• Collect samples, construct telescope and lay plaque.

The Path to Pluto

The 18-month journey to Pluto, a tiny world over three billion miles from the Sun, was truly a voyage into the unknown. No space probe had ever visited this frozen planet. It had only ever been seen by telescope – a tiny, blurred dot.

The crew's sense of excitement began to build as Pluto got closer. Tom and Yvan prepared to travel in the *Clyde* lander to Pluto's surface. There they would construct a telescope that would search for the faint heat given out by distant planets. The telescope would be powerful enough to detect not only gas giants, but also small, rocky worlds like Earth – worlds which might support life. Frozen Pluto was the ideal vantage point, because the telescope needed to be incredibly cold so no heat would confuse the readings.

THE EDGE
Pegasus finally reaches Pluto and its moon, Charon – frozen worlds, unchanged since the birth of the solar system.

Pluto

- Mostly rock, covered with ice and frozen gases. Some say it is not really a planet, but one of the Kuiper Belt objects – relics from when the planets formed.
- Diameter: 2,280 km – smaller than our Moon
- Average distance from the Sun: 5,900 million km
- Length of day: 6.38 Earth days
- Length of year: 248 Earth years
- One moon
- No rings

Far Out

As Tom and Yvan left the lander, the temperature on Pluto was -233°C.

"It's like walking round a tomb," Tom muttered, looking at his footsteps in the frozen nitrogen snow. "It's deader than dead."

It took 15 days to put the delicate telescope together. When it was ready for testing, the crew pointed the telescope at Earth. *Pegasus* picked up the image of a tiny blue ball.

"There's plenty of oxygen... water too," Nina reported. "But is there life?" She smiled at Zoë. "Maybe," she joked. "But certainly nothing intelligent!"

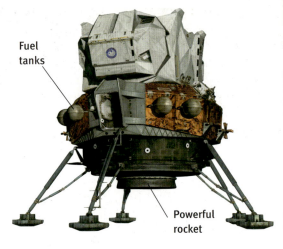

Fuel tanks

Powerful rocket

CLYDE
Named after Clyde Tombaugh, the man who discovered Pluto in 1930, the *Clyde* lander is nuclear-powered and very well-insulated. It will house a team of two on Pluto's icy surface for 15 days.

ICY WINTER
As Pluto's winter sets in and it heads for its furthest point from the Sun, the entire **atmosphere** of nitrogen freezes and falls to the surface of the planet.

> **MISSION BRIEFING**
> - Install telescope. Handling the heavy equipment will be easy, because Pluto has only 6% of the gravity of Earth.
> - Test telescope by observing Earth and checking that readings match measurements taken there.

DISTANT SUN

From Pluto the Sun looks barely bigger than a pinhead – Tom can block it out with his thumb. The Sun's light is about one hundred times brighter than the light of a full moon on Earth, just bright enough to light Pluto's surface.

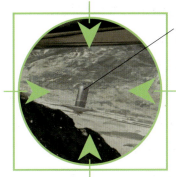

Each mirror telescope is 2 m wide.

SUPER SCOPE

The Michelson telescope uses eight mirror telescopes arranged in a large circle to make a 'combined' telescope, more powerful than any one instrument could be.

There was one more task. Tom held a special plaque in his hands, dedicated to all the men and women who had lost their lives exploring space. It was to be laid at the furthest point of *Pegasus'* journey.

Tom laid it on the frozen planet, and thought of John Pearson. Then he and Yvan shook hands.

"Let's go home," said Tom.

Secondary mirror

TRIBUTE

On the plaque that Tom laid there were 32 stars, one for each astronaut or cosmonaut who died in the course of their duty. Yvan scratched on an extra star for John.

Primary mirror

PEGASUS MISSION

WE COMMEND THE BRAVERY AND COMMITMENT OF ALL THOSE BRAVE SOULS WHO GAVE THEIR LIVES TO THE EXPLORATION OF SPACE

One More Stop

Although Tom and Yvan's departure from Pluto marked the end of the astronauts' exploration of the planets, their mission was not yet over. On the two-year trip back to Earth, *Pegasus* would pass close to the comet Yano-Moore, and Zoë and Nina faced a daunting task – to visit the comet and collect samples.

Since comets are very small and have almost no **gravity**, Nina and Zoë steered their *Messier* lander very close to the comet, and fired special cables to anchor the craft to the frozen surface. Then they put on spacesuits and jet packs – like the one Nina used in the rings of Saturn – and drifted slowly down to the black ice.

"Another first for humankind," breathed Nina, staring around at the distant stars. "Enjoying a comet's view of the universe!"

SMALL WORLD
Zoë and Nina explore the frozen surface of comet Yano-Moore. The faint glow is the first sign of dust and gas being shed.

Comet

- A comet is a chunk of dirty ice, dust and frozen gases in **orbit** around a star.
- As a comet approaches the Sun, it heats up and starts shedding dust and gas in a spectacular display. A comet's tail can stretch for millions of kilometres.
- The most famous comet seen from Earth is Halley's Comet, which returns every 76 years – it last appeared in our skies in 1985, and will next appear in 2061.

MESSIER LANDER

Messier is designed to cope with the challenges of landing on a comet. It has extra rockets built into its roof to force it down closer to the comet's surface, and fires rocket-powered harpoons into the ice to help anchor itself. Its feet are especially chilled so as not to weaken the fragile frozen surface.

The Final Test

Zoë and Nina gathered samples from the filthy black surface before returning to *Messier* for a rest period. But as they settled down, they felt the lander start to shake. Suddenly, Tom's voice burst out of *Messier's* speakers.

"The comet's breaking up! Get up and get going – now!" Nina and Zoë had barely lifted off before the comet broke open with incredible force, flinging ice in all directions.

"*Messier*, do you copy?" broadcasted Tom. There was no response – and then Tom heard an alarm, and realized *Pegasus* itself was in danger! A fragment had smashed into the cockpit, injuring Yvan and starting a fire. Desperately, Tom put it out.

And were Nina and Zoë even alive?

Luckily, *Messier's* bulletproof shielding had withstood the fierce storm of ice. As Mission Control took command of *Pegasus* and steered it out of danger, the crew worked hard to repair the damage. They were determined that nothing would stop them from getting back home.

GIANT LEAPS

The comet's **gravity** is so low that Zoë and Nina each weigh less than a pencil does on Earth. If they jumped upwards they would end up in **orbit** – and if they fell over it would take a full minute to reach the ground!

THE COMET'S TWO TAILS

The blue tail of a comet is the 'gas tail', formed from frozen gases on the surface of the comet that have vapourized in the heat of the Sun. The yellowish tail is the 'dust tail', made from great jets of dust particles. The tails always point away from the Sun – so when the comet has circled the Sun and is on the return leg of its **orbit**, its tails billow out in front of it!

Journey's End

After two weeks tending Yvan's injuries and repairing *Pegasus*, the crew were ready for the final leg of their mission. They had travelled over 11.8 billion kilometres on the adventure of a lifetime – now Earth lay just seven months and 1,440 million kilometres away. As the final weeks stretched by, it only slowly sank in that their six-year journey would soon be over.

"It'll be strange to be back on Earth again," mused Tom. "Meeting new people, breathing fresh air..."

"Walking in normal gravity," Yvan added. "Weird!"

"Maybe we should all just stay up here!" laughed Nina.

Earth

- Rocky planet
- Diameter: 12,756 km
- Average distance from the sun: 149.6 million km
- Length of day: 1 Earth day (23 hours 57 minutes)
- Length of year: 1 Earth year (365.25 Earth days)
- One moon
- No rings

As far as we know, Earth is unique: it is the only planet on which life has flourished, because its temperatures are in the right range for there to be liquid water on the surface.

But when *Pegasus* finally reached Earth, the four astronauts stared out at their blue and green world with tears in their eyes. Soon a shuttle would dock with *Pegasus*, ready to take them home. After all these years they would be back with their friends and families, free to do whatever they wanted and to go wherever they wished.

"It may have its faults," whispered Zoë, "but Earth is still my favourite planet."

GREETINGS FROM EARTH
Mission Control have sent a special greeting crew into space to dock with *Pegasus*. No one knows how the astronauts will react to company after so many years on their own, so only close friends and family, and specially-trained counsellors, will come to visit them at first.

HOMECOMING
Designed to hold 365 tonnes of water, 57 tonnes of dried food and 80 tonnes of oxygen, at last *Pegasus* has reached a place where such things are freely available – Earth!

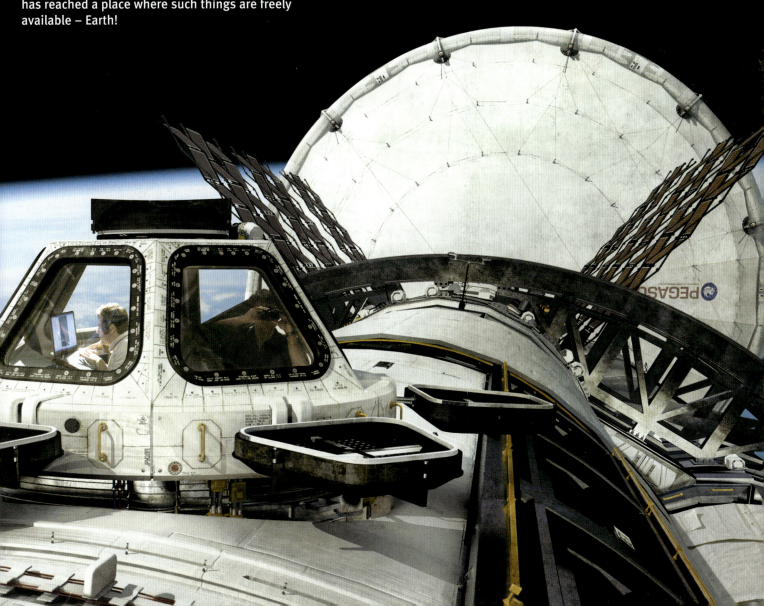

Glossary

atmosphere
The mixture of gases that surrounds a planet, moon or star.

dock
(In space) to link up one spacecraft with another.

ESA
Initials that stand for the European Space Agency, an organisation with 15 member states around Europe. Its goals are similar to those of NASA. Find out more online:
http://www.esa.int/esaCP/index.html

EVA
Initials that stand for Extra-Vehicular Activity – when an astronaut leaves a spacecraft to perform repairs, collect samples etc.

gravity
The force of attraction between every piece of matter in the universe, and every other piece. The attraction between two objects is greater the more mass they have, and it increases the closer together the objects are. Gravity is what gives us weight and what keeps the feet of someone standing on a moon or planet on the ground. It also keeps a moon in orbit around a planet or a planet in orbit around a star, stopping them from simply drifting through space.

NASA
These initials stand for the National Aeronautics and Space Administration, a US organisation dedicated to the study and exploration of space. Find out more online:
http://www.nasa.gov/home/index.html

orbit
The rotation of one celestial body (e.g. a moon) around another, larger body (e.g. a planet). The smaller body travels round and round the larger one in a predictable path, held in place by the larger one's stronger gravity. Moons orbit planets, and most planets (along with asteroids and comets) orbit stars such as our Sun. When *Pegasus* 'falls into orbit' around a planet, this means that the spaceship slows down and comes close enough to the planet to allow itself to be captured by the planet's gravity.

radiation
In this book, 'radiation' means 'ionizing radiation'. Ionizing radiation is invisible to human eyes, but travels through any space, and many substances, as rays of light do. It is dangerous because when it hits living cells, it damages the actual atoms the cells are made up of – the very substance of our bodies. The Sun pours out ionizing radiation, but Earth's atmosphere and magnetic field protect us from most of it.

solar flare
A brief but violent eruption of super-heated gases from the surface of the sun. Solar flares can reach searing temperatures of up to 100,000,000°C, and throw extra heat, light and radiation out into the solar system.